THESE 7 GORGEOUS SHAWL AND SCARF DESIGNS WILL GO TO THE TOP OF YOUR "TO CROCHET" LIST!

Designer Christine Naugle, is a stay at home mom to 3 wonderful children.

She loves the quiet time at home when she can focus on designing crochet patterns. Christine finds inspiration in the many textures and color combinations found in nature. Christine enjoys family time spent outdoors whether it be: dinning on the patio, hiking, camping, white water rafting, kayaking, snow skiing, biking or sporting events. One of her favorite places is the Sawtooth Mountains which was a big inspiration in designing the shawls and scarves found in this book. Each design was named after a lake in the Sawtooth Mountain range in central Idaho.

Christine's designs include a variety of techniques for these cozy chill-chasers, each with easy-to-follow instructions (some are also shown with step-by-step photos!). Additional photos highlight the many ways your creation may be worn. Stitched using Medium and Bulky weight yarns, these stylish wraps are great for gift-giving or just for you.

LEISURE ARTS, INC.
Maumelle, Arkansas

 **EASY**

Alturas Shawl

Finished Measurements:
18" high x 64" long (45.5 cm x 162.5 cm)

SHOPPING LIST

Yarn (Medium Weight) **MEDIUM 4**
[5.3 ounces, 481 yards
(150 grams, 440 meters) per
skein]:
☐ 2 skeins

Crochet Hook
☐ Size J (6 mm)
or size needed for gauge

Additional Supplies
☐ Yarn needle

GAUGE INFORMATION

In pattern,
12 HBdc & 9 rows = 4" (10 cm)
Gauge Swatch:
4" wide x 4¼" high
(10 cm x 10.75 cm)
Row 1: Work 12 fsc *(see
Foundation Single Crochet,
page 45)*.
Rows 2-10: Ch 2 (does **not** count
as a st), turn; HBdc in each st
across.
Finish off.

STITCH GUIDE

DOUBLE TREBLE CROCHET
(abbreviated dtr)
YO 3 times, insert hook in st indicated, YO and pull up a loop (5 loops on hook), (YO and draw through 2 loops on hook) 4 times.

HERRINGBONE DOUBLE CROCHET (abbreviated HBdc)
YO, insert hook in st indicated, YO and pull loop through st **and** through first loop on hook, YO and draw through one loop on hook, YO and draw through remaining 2 loops on hook.

SHAWL

Row 1: Work 191 fsc *(see Foundation Single Crochet, page 45)*.

Rows 2-29: Ch 2 (does **not** count as a st), turn; HBdc in each st across.

Row 30: Ch 1, turn; sc in each HBdc across.

Row 31: Ch 2 (**counts as first dc, now and throughout**), turn; dc in first sc, ch 4, skip next 4 sc, slip st in next sc, ch 4, ★ skip next 4 sc, 3 dc in next sc, ch 4, skip next 4 sc, slip st in next sc, ch 4; repeat from ★ across to last 5 sc, skip next 4 sc, 2 dc in last sc: 58 dc, 19 slip sts, and 38 ch-4 sps.

Row 32: Ch 2, turn; dc in first dc, 2 dc in next dc, ch 4, slip st in next slip st, ch 4, ★ 3 dc in next dc, dc in next dc, 3 dc in next dc, ch 4, slip st in next slip st, ch 4; repeat from ★ across to last 2 dc, 3 dc in next dc, dc in last dc: 134 dc and 38 ch-4 sps.

Row 33: Ch 2, turn; dc in first 4 dc, ch 1, skip next 2 ch-4 sps, 2 dc in next dc, ★ dc in next 5 dc, 2 dc in next dc, ch 1, skip next 2 ch-4 sps, 2 dc in next dc; repeat from ★ across to last 3 dc, dc in last 3 dc: 172 dc and 19 ch-1 sps.

Row 34: Turn; slip st in first dc, ★ ch 4, 3 dc in next ch-1 sp, ch 4, skip next 4 dc, slip st in next dc; repeat from ★ across: 57 dc, 20 slip sts, and 38 ch-4 sps.

Row 35: Turn; slip st in first slip st, ★ ch 4, 3 dc in next dc, dc in next dc, 3 dc in next dc, ch 4, slip st in next slip st; repeat from ★ across: 133 dc, 20 slip sts, and 38 ch-4 sps.

Row 36: Ch 6 (**counts as first dtr plus ch 1**), turn; skip next ch-4 sp, 2 dc in next dc, dc in next 5 dc, 2 dc in next dc, ch 1, ★ skip next 2 ch-4 sps, 2 dc in next dc, dc in next 5 dc, 2 dc in next dc, ch 1; repeat from ★ across to last slip st, dtr in last slip st: 171 dc, 2 dtr, and 20 ch-1 sps.

Row 37: Ch 2, turn; dc in next ch-1 sp, ch 4, skip next 4 dc, slip st in next dc, ch 4, skip next 4 dc, ★ 3 dc in next ch-1 sp, ch 4, skip next 4 dc, slip st in next dc, ch 4, skip next 4 dc; repeat from ★ across to last ch-1 sp, dc in last ch-1 sp and in last dtr: 58 dc, 19 slip sts, and 38 ch-4 sps.

Rows 38 and 39: Repeat Rows 32 and 33: 172 dc and 19 ch-1 sps.

Row 40 (Right side)**:** Ch 1, turn; sc in each dc and in each ch-1 sp across; finish off.

Imogene Infinity Cowl

Finished Measurements:
8½" wide x 82" long (before sewing) (21.5 cm x 208.5 cm)

SHOPPING LIST

Yarn (Bulky Weight)
[5.3 ounces, 312 yards
(150 grams, 285 meters) per
skein]:
- ☐ 2 skeins

Crochet Hook
- ☐ Size J (6 mm)
  or size needed for gauge

Additional Supplies
- ☐ Yarn needle

GAUGE INFORMATION

13 dc and 7 rows = 4" (10 cm)
3 pattern repeats = 7½"
   (19 cm) wide
Gauge Swatch: 4" (10 cm) square
Ch 15.
Row 1: Dc in fourth ch from hook
(3 skipped chs count as first dc)
and in each ch across: 13 dc.
Rows 2-7: Ch 3 **(counts as first
dc)**, turn; dc in next dc and in each
dc across.
Finish off.

STITCH GUIDE

PUFF STITCH

(abbreviated Puff St)

(uses one st)

★ YO, insert hook in st indicated, YO and pull up a loop even with loop on hook; repeat from ★ 2 times **more** (7 loops on hook), YO and draw through 6 loops on hook, YO and draw through remaining 2 loops on hook.

COWL

Ch 34.

Row 1 (Right side)**:** Sc in second ch from hook and in next 2 chs, ★ ch 5, skip next 3 chs, slip st in next ch, ch 5, skip next 3 chs, sc in next 3 chs; repeat from ★ 2 times **more**: 12 sc and 6 ch-5 sps.

Row 2: Ch 2 (**counts as dc, now and throughout**), turn; work Puff St in next sc, dc in next sc, ★ ch 2, slip st in next ch-5 sp, ch 5, slip st in next ch-5 sp, ch 2, dc in next sc, work Puff St in next sc, dc in next sc; repeat from ★ 2 times **more**: 8 dc, 4 Puff Sts, and 9 sps.

Row 3: Ch 1, turn; sc in first 3 sts, ★ ch 5, skip next ch-2 sp, slip st in next ch-5 sp, ch 5, skip next ch-2 sp, sc in next 3 sts; repeat from ★ 2 times **more**: 12 sc and 6 ch-5 sps.

Row 4: Ch 2, turn; work Puff St in next sc, dc in next sc, ★ ch 2, slip st in next ch-5 sp, ch 5, slip st in next ch-5 sp, ch 2, dc in next sc, work Puff St in next sc, dc in next sc; repeat from ★ 2 times **more**: 8 dc, 4 Puff Sts, and 9 sps.

Repeat Rows 3 and 4 for pattern until piece measures approximately 82" (208.5 cm) from beginning ch, ending by working Row 4.

Finish off leaving a long end for sewing.

Being careful **not** to twist piece, fold Scarf in half with **right** side together and matching last row with beginning ch. Thread yarn needle with long end and sew ends together.

■■■▣ **INTERMEDIATE**

Toxaway Shawl

Finished Measurements: 21" high x 60" (53.5 cm x 152.5 cm) (before sewing) 21" high x 30" wide (53.5 cm x 76 cm) (sewn)

SHOPPING LIST

Yarn (Medium Weight) 🄴4🄴

[5 ounces, 250 yards (141 grams, 228 meters) per skein]:
- ☐ Off White - 3 skeins
- ☐ Brown - 2 skeins

[6 ounces, 315 yards (170 grams, 288 meters) per skein]:
- ☐ Orange - 1 skein

Crochet Hook
- ☐ Size I (5.5 mm)
  or size needed for gauge

Additional Supplies
- ☐ Ruler - about 1¹⁄₈" high and 12" or longer in length (3 cm x 30.5 cm)

Note: The height of your ruler will affect the final size of your shawl.
- ☐ Clothespins - 2 (to hold sts at each end of ruler)
- ☐ Yarn needle

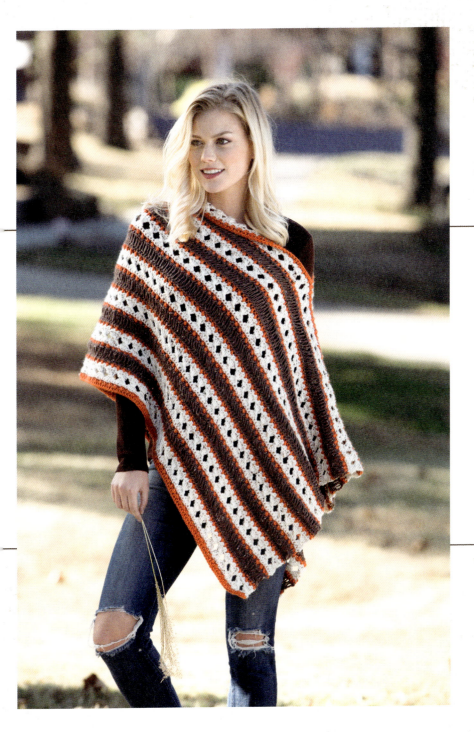

GAUGE INFORMATION

16 sc and 20 rows = 4" (10 cm)

Gauge Swatch: 4" (10 cm) square

Ch 17.

Row 1: Sc in second ch from hook and in each ch across: 16 sc.

Rows 2-20: Ch 1, turn; sc in each sc across.

Finish off.

STITCH GUIDE

MINI BEAN *(abbreviated MB)*

(uses one st)

Insert hook in st indicated, YO and pull up a loop (2 loops on hook), YO, insert hook in **same** st, YO and pull up a loop, YO and draw through all 4 loops on hook.

Fig. A

DOUBLE CROCHET 3 TOGETHER

(abbreviated dc3tog) (uses next 3 sts)

★ YO, insert hook in **next** st, YO and pull up a loop, YO and draw through 2 loops on hook; repeat from ★ 2 times **more**, YO and draw through all 4 loops on hook.

Fig. B

BEGINNING EXTENDED CROSS STITCH

(abbreviated beg ex Cross St)

(uses first 4 sts)

Ch 2 (**counts as first st**), skip first st, dc3tog, ch 2, 3 dc in top of dc3tog *(Figs. A & B)*.

Fig. C

EXTENDED CROSS STITCH

(abbreviated ex Cross St)

(uses next 4 sts)

YO 3 times, insert hook in next st, YO and pull up a loop, YO and draw through 2 loops (4 loops on hook), ★ YO, insert hook in **next** st, YO and pull up a loop, YO and draw through 2 loops on hook; repeat from ★ 2 times **more** (7 loops on hook), YO and draw through 5 loops on hook (3 loops on hook), (YO and draw through 2 loops on hook) twice, 3 dc in top of st just made *(Figs. C & D)*.

Fig. D

SHAWL

Row 1: With Orange, work 228 fsc *(see Foundation Single Crochet, page 45)*.

Row 2 (Right side)**:** Ch 1, turn; work MB in next st, ★ ch 1, skip next st, work MB in next st; repeat from ★ across to last st, hdc in last st; finish off: 114 MB, one hdc, and 113 chs.

Note: Loop a short piece of yarn around any stitch to mark Row 2 as **right** side.

Row 3: With **wrong** side facing, join Off White with sc in first hdc *(see Joining With Sc, page 45)*; sc in each MB and in each ch across: 228 sc.

Row 4: Turn; work beg ex Cross St, work ex Cross Sts across: 57 ex Cross Sts.

Row 5: Ch 1, turn; sc in first 3 sts, sc in sp **before** next ex Cross St *(Fig. 5, page 46)*, (sc in next 3 sts, sc in sp **before** next ex Cross St) across to last ex Cross St, sc in last 4 sts changing to Orange in last sc *(Fig. 3a, page 46)*; cut Off White: 228 sc.

Row 6: Ch 1, turn; work MB in next sc, ★ ch 1, skip next sc, work MB in next sc; repeat from ★ across to last sc, hdc in last sc; finish off: 114 MB, one hdc, and 113 chs.

Row 7: With **wrong** side facing, join Brown with sc in first hdc; sc in each MB and in each ch across: 228 sc.

Row 8:

First Half - Turn; pull up loop on hook and place on ruler *(Fig. E)*, clip a clothespin on the opposite end of ruler to keep loops from sliding off, ★ insert hook in next sc, YO and pull up a loop and place on ruler; repeat from ★ across (it will be a tight fit but all loops will fit on one ruler), clip second clothespin on end of ruler to hold loops on ruler *(Fig. F)*: 228 loops.

Fig. E

Fig. F

Second Half - Turn; remove clothespin and insert hook into first loop on ruler, make a loose ch *(Fig. G)*, sc in same loop, sc in each loop on ruler *(Fig. H)* pulling the loops off of ruler as you work and changing to Orange in last sc; cut Brown: 228 sc.

Fig. G

Fig. H

Row 9: Ch 1, turn; work MB in next sc, ★ ch 1, skip next sc, work MB in next sc; repeat from ★ across to last sc, hdc in last sc; finish off: 114 MB, one hdc, and 113 chs.

Rows 10-44: Repeat Rows 3-9, 5 times [Shawl will measure about 20" (51 cm) high]: 114 MB, one hdc, and 113 chs.

Rows 45-48: Repeat Rows 3-6; at end of Row 48, do **not** finish off Orange.

Row 49: Ch 1, turn; working in each st and in each ch, sc in first 65 sts, place marker in last sc made for assembly, sc in next 98 sts, slip st in next st, finish off leaving a 36" (91.5 cm) length for sewing of yarn.

With **right** side facing, match first and last 65 sts of Row 49 so they are side by side. Thread yarn needle with end and using mattress stitch *(Figs. 6a & b, page 47)*, sew the unworked stitches together with the first 65 sc of your final row, beginning at marked st and working down to the beginning of the row. This creates the seam down the shoulder of the shawl.

◖◼☐◗ EASY

Alpine Scarf

Finished Measurements:
28" deep (width at point) x 60" wingspan (top edge) (71 cm x 152.5 cm)

SHOPPING LIST

Yarn (Medium Weight) 🔴4🔴
[5 ounces, 251 yards
(142 grams, 230 meters) per skein]:
☐ Green - 3 skeins
☐ Tan - 1 skein

Crochet Hook
☐ Size J (6 mm)
   or size needed for gauge

Additional Supplies
☐ Yarn needle

GAUGE INFORMATION

In pattern,

   13 exsc and 11 rows = 4" (10 cm)

Gauge Swatch: 4" (10 cm) square
Ch 15.

Row 1: Exsc in third ch from hook
and in each ch across: 13 exsc.

Rows 2-11: Ch 1, turn; exsc in
each exsc across.
Finish off.

STITCH GUIDE

EXTENDED SINGLE CROCHET
   (abbreviated exsc)

Pull up a loop in st indicated,
YO and draw through one loop
on hook, YO and draw through
remaining 2 loops on hook.

SCARF

Row 1: With Tan, ch 4, working in back ridge of chs *(Fig. 1, page 45)*, (sc, dc) in second ch from hook, skip next ch, (sc, dc) in last ch: 4 sts.

Row 2 (Right side)**:** Ch 2, turn; working in Back Loops Only *(Fig. 2, page 46)*, skip first dc, (sc, dc) in next sc, skip next dc, (sc, dc) in last dc.

Row 3: Ch 1, turn; working in BLO, skip first dc, ★ (sc, dc) in next sc, skip next dc; repeat ★ once **more**, (sc, dc) in top of turning ch: 6 sts.

Row 4: Ch 2, turn; working in BLO, skip first dc, (sc, dc) in next sc, ★ skip next dc, (sc, dc) in next sc; repeat from ★ once **more**.

Row 5: Ch 1, turn; working in BLO, skip first dc, ★ (sc, dc) in next sc, skip next dc; repeat from ★ 2 times **more**, (sc, dc) in top of turning ch: 8 sts.

Row 6: Ch 2, turn; working in BLO, skip first dc, (sc, dc) in next sc, ★ skip next dc, (sc, dc) in next sc; repeat from ★ 2 times **more**, changing to Green in last dc *(Fig. 3b, page 46)*; cut Tan.

Row 7 (Increase row)**:** Ch 1, turn; working in both loops, exsc in first dc and in each st across to last sc, 2 exsc in last sc: 9 exsc.

Row 8 (Increase row)**:** Ch 2, turn; 2 exsc in first st, exsc in next st and in each st across changing to Tan in last exsc; cut Green: 10 exsc.

Row 9 (Increase row)**:** Ch 1, turn; working in BLO, skip first st, (sc, dc) in next st, ★ skip next st, (sc, dc) in next st; repeat from ★ across, (sc, dc) in top of turning ch: 12 sts.

Row 10: Ch 2, turn; working in BLO, skip first dc, (sc, dc) in next sc, ★ skip next dc, (sc, dc) in next sc; repeat from ★ across.

Rows 11 and 12: Repeat Rows 9 and 10, changing to Green in last dc on Row 12; cut Tan: 14 sts.

Row 13 (Increase row)**:** Ch 1, turn; working in both loops, exsc in first dc and in each st across to last sc, 2 exsc in last sc: 15 exsc.

Row 14 (Increase row)**:** Ch 2, turn; 2 exsc in first st, exsc in next st and in each st across changing to Tan in last exsc; cut Green: 16 exsc.

Row 15: Ch 1, turn; working in BLO, skip first st, (sc, dc) in next st, ★ skip next st, (sc, dc) in next st; repeat from ★ across, (sc, dc) in top of turning ch: 18 sts.

Row 16: Ch 2, turn; working in BLO, skip first dc, (sc, dc) in next sc, ★ skip next dc, (sc, dc) in next sc; repeat from ★ across changing to Green in last dc, cut Tan.

Row 17: Ch 1, turn; working in both loops, exsc in first dc and in each st across to last sc, 2 exsc in last sc: 19 sts.

Row 18 (Increase row)**:** Ch 2, turn; 2 exsc in first st, exsc in next st and in each st across: 20 exsc.

Row 19 (Increase row)**:** Ch 1, turn; exsc in first exsc and in each exsc across to last exsc, 2 exsc in last exsc: 21 exsc.

Rows 20-111: Repeat Rows 18 and 19, 46 times: 113 exsc.

Row 112: Ch 2, turn; 2 exsc in first st, exsc in next st and in each st across, changing to Tan in last exsc; cut Green: 114 sts.

Row 113: Ch 1, turn; working in BLO, skip first st, (sc, dc) in next st, ★ skip next st, (sc, dc) in next st; repeat from ★ across, (sc, dc) in top of turning ch: 116 sts.

Row 114: Ch 2, turn; working in BLO, skip first dc, (sc, dc) in next sc, ★ skip next dc, (sc, dc) in next sc; repeat from ★ across changing to Green in last dc, cut Tan.

Rows 115-122: Repeat Rows 7-14: 124 exsc.

Row 123 (Increase row)**:** Ch 1, turn; working in BLO, skip first st, (sc, dc) in next st, ★ skip next st, (sc, dc) in next st; repeat from ★ across, (sc, dc) in top of turning ch: 126 sts.

Row 124: Ch 2, turn; working in BLO, skip first dc, (sc, dc) in next sc, ★ skip next dc, (sc, dc) in next sc; repeat from ★ across.

Rows 125-128: Repeat Rows 123 and 124 twice: 130 sts.

Finish off.

Trail Creek Neck Warmer

EASY +

Finished Measurements:
5½" wide x 27" long (14 cm x 68.5 cm)

SHOPPING LIST
Yarn
(Medium Weight)
[5 ounces, 280 yards
(140 grams, 256 meters) per
skein]:
☐ Variegated - 1 skein

(Bulky Weight)
[3.5 ounces, 101 yards
(100 grams, 92 meters) per
skein]:
☐ Off White - 1 skein

Crochet Hook
☐ Size I (5.5 mm)
or size needed for gauge

Additional Supplies
☐ Yarn needle
☐ ¾" (19 mm) Buttons - 2

GAUGE INFORMATION
In pattern,
    13 sc and 16 rows = 4" (10 cm)
Gauge Swatch: 4" (10 cm) square
Row 1: With Variegated, work
13 fsc *(see Foundation Single
Crochet, page 45)*.
Rows 2-16: Ch 1, turn; sc in each
st across.
Finish off.

STITCH GUIDE

FRONT POST PUFF STITCH
   (abbreviated FP Puff St) (uses one st)
★ YO, insert hook from **front** to **back** around post of st indicated *(Fig. 4, page 46)*, YO and pull up a loop even with loop on hook; repeat from ★ once **more**, YO and draw through all 5 loops on hook.

FRONT POST SINGLE CROCHET
   (abbreviated FPsc) (uses one st)
Insert hook from **front** to **back** around post of st indicated *(Fig. 4, page 46)*, YO and pull up a loop, YO and draw through both loops on hook.

SINGLE CROCHET 2 TOGETHER *(abbreviated sc2tog)*
Pull up a loop in each of next 2 sts, YO and draw through all 3 loops on hook **(counts as one sc)**.

NECK WARMER
Outer Section

The Outer section tends to curl as you crochet. This will be corrected as you crochet the Border.

Row 1 (Right side)**:** With Variegated, work 17 fsc *(see Foundation Single Crochet, page 45)*.

Note: Loop a short piece of yarn around any stitch to mark Row 1 as **right** side.

Row 2: Ch 1, turn; sc in each st across.

Row 3: Ch 2 (does **not** count as a st), turn; dc in first 2 sc, ch 1, skip next sc **(buttonhole made)**, dc in last 14 sc: 16 dc and one ch.

Row 4: Ch 1, turn; sc in each dc and ch across: 17 sc.

Row 5: Ch 1, turn; sc in first sc, (work FP Puff St around next sc, sc in next 3 sc) across.

Row 6: Ch 1, turn; sc in each st across.

Row 7: Ch 1, turn; sc in first 3 sc, work FP Puff St around first FP Puff St 2 rows **below**, skip next sc from last sc made, ★ sc in next 3 sc, work FP Puff St around next FP Puff St 2 rows **below**, skip next sc from last sc made; repeat from ★ once **more**, sc in last sc.

Row 8: Ch 1, turn; sc in each st across.

Row 9: Ch 1, turn; sc in first sc, work FP Puff St around next sc, sc in next 3 sc, ★ work FP Puff St around next FP Puff St 2 rows **below**, skip next sc from last sc made, sc in next 3 sc; repeat from ★ 2 times **more**.

Rows 10-99: Repeat Rows 6-9, 22 times; then repeat Rows 6 and 7 once **more**.

Rows 100-102: Ch 1, turn; sc in each st across.

BORDER

Rnd 1 (Right side)**:** Turn; slip st in each sc across, ch 1; working in end of rows, sc in each sc row across working 2 sc in end of Row 3 (dc row), ch 1; slip st in ch at base of each fsc on Row 1, ch 1; working in end of rows, sc in each sc row across working 2 sc in end of Row 3 (dc row), ch 1; join with slip st to first slip st: 244 sts (206 sc, 34 slip sts, and 4 chs).

Rnd 2: Turn; slip st in first 4 sts, work FPsc around each of next 97 sc, slip st in next 4 sts; slip st in Front Loops Only of next 17 slip sts *(Fig. 2, page 46)*; slip st in **both** loops of next 4 sts, place a marker in last slip st made for Inner Lining placement, work FPsc around each of next 97 sc, slip st in next st, place a marker in st just made for Inner Lining placement, slip st in next 3 sts; slip st in Front Loops Only of last 17 slip sts; join with slip st to **both** loops of first slip st, finish off.

Inner Lining

Row 1: With **wrong** side facing, join Off White with slip st in first marked st, remove marker; (sc in next st, sc2tog) across ending in next marked st, remove marker: 65 sc.

Row 2 (Right side)**:** Ch 2, turn; dc in first sc, ★ ch 1, skip next sc, dc in next sc; repeat from ★ across: 33 dc and 32 ch-1 sps.

Note: Mark Row 2 as **right** side.

Rows 3-9: Ch 2, turn; skip first dc, dc in next ch-1 sp, ch 1, ★ skip next dc, dc in next ch-1 sp, ch 1; repeat from ★ across to last dc, dc in last dc.

Row 10 (Joining row)**:** Turn; with **wrong** sides of Inner Lining and Outer Section together, slip st in fourth st on opposite Border of Outer Section; ch 1, working through both layers, sc in first dc of Inner Lining **and** corresponding st of Border, ★ working in ch-1 sp of Inner Lining and next 2 sts of Border, sc2tog, sc in next dc of Inner Lining **and** next st of Border; repeat from ★ across; finish off.

Sew buttons to **right** side of Outer Section (on 2nd and 16th sts of Row 101).

 **EASY +**

Trinity Capelet

Size: One Size Fits Most
Finished Measurements:
Neck Opening: 22" (56 cm) circumference
Bottom Opening: 48¾" (124 cm) circumference
Total Length: 13" (33 cm)

SHOPPING LIST

Yarn (Bulky Weight) 🧶 **5**
[3.5 ounces, 147 yards
(100 grams, 134 meters) per
skein]:
☐ Gold - 3 skeins
☐ Lt Grey - 1 skein

Crochet Hook
☐ Size J (6 mm)
   or size needed for gauge

Additional Supplies
☐ Split-ring markers - 2
☐ Safety pin
☐ Yarn needle

GAUGE INFORMATION

12 sc and 15 rows = 4" (10 cm)
In pattern, 6 Tsts = 4" (10 cm);
   8 rows = 3¾" (9.5 cm)
Gauge Swatch: 4" (10 sc) square
Ch 13.
Row 1: Sc in second ch from hook
and in each ch across: 12 sc.
Rows 2-15: Ch 1, turn; sc in each
sc across.
Finish off.

STITCH GUIDE

TRIANGLE STITCH *(abbreviated Tst)* (uses next 2 sc)

YO, insert hook in same st as last st worked into, YO and pull up a loop (3 loops on hook) *(Fig. A)*, (YO, insert hook in **next** sc, YO and pull up a loop) twice (7 loops on hook) *(Fig. B)*, YO and draw through 6 loops on hook *(Fig. C)*, YO and draw through remaining 2 loops on hook, ch 1 *(Fig. D)*.

Fig. A

Fig. B

Fig. C

Fig. D

EXTENDED SINGLE CROCHET *(abbreviated exsc)*

Insert hook in st indicated, YO and pull up a loop even with loop on hook, YO and draw through both loops on hook.

CAPELET

Rnd 1 (Right side)**:** With Gold, work 66 fsc *(see Foundation Single Crochet, page 45)*; being careful not to twist piece, join with slip st to first fsc.

Rnd 2: Ch 1, sc in same st as joining and in each fsc around; join with slip st to first sc.

Rnd 3 (Right side)**:** Ch 2, beginning in same st as joining, work 11 Tsts, place marker around last Tst made, work 6 Tsts, place marker around last Tst made, work Tsts around ending last Tst in same st as first Tst was worked into; skip beginning ch-2 and join with slip st to top of first Tst, place loop from hook onto safety pin to keep piece from unraveling while working Contrasting Section: 33 Tsts.

Rnd 3 - Contrasting Section:
With **right** side facing and beginning at first marker, join Lt Grey with exsc in first sc that marked Tst worked into; ★ skip Tst, work (exsc, ch 1, exsc) in first sc that next Tst worked into; repeat from ★ 5 times **more**, skip Tst, work exsc in first sc that next Tst worked into, pull up a long loop and drop Lt Grey to **wrong** side until needed, remove stitch markers, place Gold loop from safety pin onto hook.

Lt Grey will be carried on the **wrong** side of the piece.

Rnd 4: Ch 1, turn; 2 sc in ch-1 sp of each Tst around working **over** ch-1 of Contrasting Section; join with slip st to first sc: 66 sc.

Rnd 5: Ch 2, turn; work 11 Tsts, place marker around last Tst made, work 6 Tsts, place marker around last Tst made, work Tsts around ending last Tst in same st as first Tst was worked into; skip beginning ch-2 and join with slip st to top of first Tst, place loop from hook onto safety pin to keep piece from unraveling while working Contrasting Section: 33 Tsts.

Rnd 5 - Contrasting Section: With **right** side facing, insert hook in last sc that last marked Tst worked into, pull Lt Grey loop up to height of marked Tst, slip st in top of marked Tst, ch 1, **turn**; ★ skip Tst, work (exsc, ch 1, exsc) in first sc that next Tst worked into; repeat from ★ 5 times **more**, skip Tst, work exsc in first sc that next Tst worked into, pull up a long loop and drop Lt Grey to **wrong** side until needed, remove stitch markers, place Gold loop from safety pin onto hook.

Rnd 6: Ch 1, turn; 2 sc in ch-1 sp of each Tst around working **over** ch-1 of Contrasting Section; join with slip st to first sc: 66 sc.

Rnd 7: Ch 2, turn; beginning in same st as joining, work 11 Tsts, place marker around last Tst made, work 6 Tsts, place marker around last Tst made, work Tsts around ending last Tst in same st as first Tst was worked into; skip beginning ch-2 and join with slip st to top of first Tst, place loop from hook onto safety pin to keep piece from unraveling while working Contrasting Section: 33 Tsts.

Rnd 7 - Contrasting Section:
With **right** side facing, insert hook in first sc that marked Tst worked into, pull Lt Grey loop up to height of marked Tst, slip st in top of marked Tst, ★ skip Tst, work (exsc, ch 1, exsc) in first sc that next Tst worked into; repeat from ★ 5 times **more**, skip Tst, work exsc in first sc that next Tst worked into, pull up a long loop and drop Lt Grey to **wrong** side until needed, remove stitch markers, place Gold loop from safety pin onto hook.

Rnds 8-11: Repeat Rnds 4-7.

Rnd 12: Ch 1, turn; 3 sc in ch-1 sp of each Tst around to last Tst working **over** ch-1 of Contrasting Section, 2 sc in last ch-1 sp; join with slip st to first sc: 98 sc.

Rnd 13: Ch 2, turn; beginning in same st as joining, work 16 Tsts, place marker around last Tst made, work 8 Tsts, place marker around last Tst made, work Tsts around ending last Tst in same st as first Tst was worked into; skip beginning ch-2 and join with slip st to top of first Tst, place loop from hook onto safety pin to keep piece from unraveling while working Contrasting Section: 49 Tsts.

Rnd 13 - Contrasting Section:
With **right** side facing, insert hook in last sc that last marked Tst worked into, pull Lt Grey loop up to height of marked Tst, slip st in top of marked Tst, ch 1, **turn**; ★ skip Tst, work (exsc, ch 1, exsc) in first sc that next Tst worked into; repeat from ★ 7 times **more**, skip Tst, work exsc in first sc that next Tst worked into, pull up a long loop and drop Lt Grey to **wrong** side until needed, remove stitch markers, place Gold loop from safety pin onto hook.

Rnd 14: Ch 1, turn; 3 sc in ch-1 sp of each Tst around to last Tst working **over** ch-1 of Contrasting Section, 2 sc in last ch-1 sp; join with slip st to first sc: 146 sc.

Row 15: Ch 2, turn; beginning in same st as joining, work 24 Tsts, place marker around last Tst made, work 11 Tsts, place marker around last Tst made, work Tsts around ending last Tst in same st

as first Tst was worked into; skip beginning ch-2 and join with slip st to top of first Tst, place loop from hook onto safety pin to keep piece from unraveling while working Contrasting Section: 73 Tsts.

Rnd 15 - Contrasting Section:
With **right** side facing, insert hook in first sc that marked Tst worked into, pull Lt Grey loop up to height of marked Tst, slip st in top of marked Tst, ★ skip Tst, work (exsc, ch 1, exsc) in first sc that next Tst worked into; repeat from ★ 10 times **more**, skip Tst, work exsc in first sc that next Tst worked into, pull up a long loop and drop Lt Grey to **wrong** side until needed, remove stitch markers, place Gold loop from safety pin onto hook.

Rnd 16: Ch 1, turn; 2 sc in ch-1 sp of each Tst around working **over** ch-1 of Contrasting Section; join with slip st to first sc: 146 sc.

Rnd 17: Ch 2, turn; beginning in same st as joining, work 24 Tsts, place marker around last Tst made, work 11 Tsts, place marker around last Tst made, work Tsts around ending last Tst in same st as first Tst was worked into; skip beginning ch-2 and join with slip st to top of first Tst, place loop from hook onto safety pin to keep piece from unraveling while working Contrasting Section: 73 Tsts.

Rnd 17 - Contrasting Section: With **right** side facing, insert hook in last sc that last marked Tst worked into, pull Lt Grey loop up to height of marked Tst, slip st in top of marked Tst, ch 1, **turn**; ★ skip Tst, work (exsc, ch 1, exsc) in first sc that next Tst worked into; repeat from ★ 10 times **more**, skip Tst, work exsc in first sc that next Tst worked into, pull up a long loop and drop Lt Grey to **wrong** side until needed, remove stitch markers, place Gold loop from safety pin onto hook.

Rnd 18: Ch 1, turn; 2 sc in ch-1 sp of each Tst around working **over** ch-1 of Contrasting Section; join with slip st to first sc: 146 sc.

Rnd 19-28: Repeat Rnds 15-18 twice, then repeat Rnds 15 and 16 once **more**; at end of Rnd 27, finish off Lt Grey.

Rnd 29: Ch 1, turn; sc in same st as joining and in each sc around; join with slip st to first sc, finish off.

Twin Lakes Infinity Scarf

EASY

Finished Measurements:
5" wide x 70" long (before sewing) (12.5 cm x 178 cm)

SHOPPING LIST

Yarn (Medium Weight) 🄸4
[16 ounces, 867 yards
(454 grams, 792 meters) per
skein]:
- ☐ White - 330 yards
  (302 meters)
- ☐ Blue - 330 yards (302 meters)

Crochet Hook
- ☐ Size I (5.5 mm)
  or size needed for gauge

Additional Supplies
- ☐ Yarn needle

GAUGE INFORMATION

In pattern,
   12 dc and 8 rows = 4" (10 cm)
Gauge Swatch: 4" (10 cm) square
Ch 14.
Row 1: Dc in fourth ch from hook
(3 skipped chs count as first dc)
and in each ch across: 12 dc.
Rows 2-8: Ch 3 **(counts as first
dc)**, turn; dc in next dc and in each
dc across.
Finish off.

STITCH GUIDE

DOUBLE CROCHET
2 TOGETHER
(abbreviated dc2tog)
(uses next ch-1 sp and last dc)
YO, insert hook in next ch-1 sp,
YO and pull up a loop, YO and
draw through 2 loops on hook,
YO, insert hook in last dc, YO
and pull up a loop, YO and draw
through 2 loops on hook, YO
and draw through all 3 loops on
hook **(counts as one dc)**.

SCARF
Strip
(Make one White & one Blue)
With color indicated, ch 23.

Row 1: Dc in third ch from hook,
(ch 1, skip next 2 chs, 2 dc in next
ch) 3 times, ch 2, 2 dc in next ch,
(ch 1, skip next 2 chs, 2 dc in next
ch) twice, ch 1, skip next 2 chs,
(YO, insert hook in **next** ch, YO
and pull up a loop, YO and draw
through 2 loops on hook) twice,
YO and draw through all 3 loops
on hook **(counts as one dc)**: 14 dc
and 7 sps.

Rows 2-124: Ch 2, turn; dc in next
ch-1 sp, ch 1, (2 dc in next ch-1 sp,
ch 1) twice, (2 dc, ch 2, 2 dc) in
next ch-2 sp, ch 1, (2 dc in next
ch-1 sp, ch 1) twice, dc2tog.

Finish off leaving a long end for
sewing.

Fold both Strips in half having
one fold on top of the other (folds
will be facing opposite directions)
(Fig. A).

Fig. A

Bring top Strip ends up through the bottom fold *(Fig. B)*.

Fig. B

Repeat, bringing ends through same loop once **more** *(Fig. C)*.

Fig. C

Pull ends to tighten *(Fig. D)*.

Fig. D

Bring the end of Strips together, aligning points with indented ends *(Fig. E)* and sew together.

Fig. E

General Instructions

ABBREVIATIONS

beg	beginning
BLO	Back Loop(s) Only
ch(s)	chain(s)
cm	centimeters
dc	double crochet(s)
dc2tog	double crochet 2 together
dc3tog	double crochet 3 together
dtr	double treble crochet(s)
ex	extended
exsc	extended single crochet(s)
FP	Front Post
FPsc	Front Post single crochet(s)
fsc	foundation single crochet(s)
HBdc	herringbone double crochet(s)
hdc	half double crochet(s)
MB	Mini Bean
mm	millimeters
PP	puff post stitch
sc	single crochet(s)
sc2tog	single crochet 2 together
sp(s)	space(s)
st(s)	stitch(es)
Tst(s)	Triangle stitch(es)
YO	yarn over

SYMBOLS & TERMS

★ — work instructions following ★ as many **more** times as indicated in addition to the first time.

( ) or **[ ]** — work enclosed instructions **as many** times as indicated in addition to the first time **or** work all enclosed instructions in the stitch or space indicated **or** contains explanatory remarks.

colon (:) — the number(s) given after a colon at the end of a row or round denote(s) the number of stitches or spaces you should have on that row or round.

CROCHET TERMINOLOGY	
UNITED STATES	INTERNATIONAL
slip stitch (slip st) =	single crochet (sc)
single crochet (sc) =	double crochet (dc)
half double crochet (hdc) =	half treble crochet (htr)
double crochet (dc) =	treble crochet (tr)
treble crochet (tr) =	double treble crochet (dtr)
double treble crochet (dtr) =	triple treble crochet (ttr)
triple treble crochet (tr tr) =	quadruple treble crochet (qtr)
skip =	miss

GAUGE

Exact gauge is essential for proper size. Before beginning your project, make the sample swatch given in the individual instructions in the yarn and hook specified. After completing the swatch, measure it, counting your stitches and rows/rounds carefully. If your swatch is larger or smaller than specified, **make another, changing hook size to get the correct gauge**. Keep trying until you find the size hook that will give you the specified gauge.

Yarn Weight Symbol & Names	LACE 0	SUPER FINE 1	FINE 2	LIGHT 3	MEDIUM 4	BULKY 5	SUPER BULKY 6	JUMBO 7
Type of Yarns in Category	Fingering, size 10 crochet thread	Sock, Fingering, Baby	Sport, Baby	DK, Light Worsted	Worsted, Afghan, Aran	Chunky, Craft, Rug	Super Bulky, Roving	Jumbo, Roving
Crochet Gauge* Ranges in Single Crochet to 4" (10 cm)	32-42 sts**	21-32 sts	16-20 sts	12-17 sts	11-14 sts	8-11 sts	6-9 sts	5 sts and fewer
Advised Hook Size Range	Steel*** 6 to 8, Regular hook B-1	B-1 to E-4	E-4 to 7	7 to I-9	I-9 to K-10½	K-10½ to M/N-13	M/N-13 to Q	Q and larger

*GUIDELINES ONLY: The chart above reflects the most commonly used gauges and hook sizes for specific yarn categories.

** Lace weight yarns are usually crocheted with larger hooks to create lacy openwork patterns. Accordingly, a gauge range is difficult to determine. Always follow the gauge stated in your pattern.

*** Steel crochet hooks are sized differently from regular hooks–the higher the number, the smaller the hook, which is the reverse of regular hook sizing.

■□□□ BEGINNER	Projects for first-time crocheters using basic stitches. Minimal shaping.
■■□□ EASY	Projects using yarn with basic stitches, repetitive stitch patterns, simple color changes, and simple shaping and finishing.
■■■□ INTERMEDIATE	Projects using a variety of techniques, such as basic lace patterns or color patterns, mid-level shaping and finishing.
■■■■ EXPERIENCED	Projects with intricate stitch patterns, techniques and dimension, such as non-repeating patterns, multi-color techniques, fine threads, small hooks, detailed shaping and refined finishing.

JOINING WITH SC

When instructed to join with sc, begin with a slip knot on hook. Insert hook in stitch or space indicated, YO and pull up a loop, YO and draw through both loops on hook.

FOUNDATION SINGLE CROCHET *(abbreviated fsc)*

Ch 2, insert hook in second ch from hook, YO and pull up a loop, YO and draw through one loop on hook (**ch made**), YO and draw through both loops on hook (**first fsc made**), ★ insert hook in ch at base of last fsc made, YO and pull up a loop, YO and draw through one loop on hook (**ch made**), YO and draw through both loops on hook (**fsc made**); repeat from ★ for each additional fsc.

BACK RIDGE OF A CHAIN

Work only in loops indicated by arrows *(Fig. 1)*.

Fig. 1

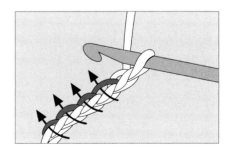

CROCHET HOOKS	
U.S.	**Metric mm**
B-1	2.25
C-2	2.75
D-3	3.25
E-4	3.5
F-5	3.75
G-6	4
7	4.5
H-8	5
I-9	5.5
J-10	6
K-10½	6.5
L-11	8
M/N-13	9
N/P-15	10
P/Q	15
Q	16
S	19

BACK OR FRONT LOOP ONLY

Work only in loop(s) indicated by arrow (*Fig. 2*).

Fig. 2

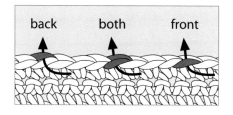

POST STITCH

Work around post of stitch indicated, inserting hook in direction of arrow (*Fig. 4*).

Fig. 4

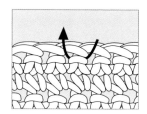

CHANGING COLORS

Work the last stitch to within one step of completion, hook new yarn (*Fig. 3a or 3b*) and draw through both loops on hook.

Fig. 3a

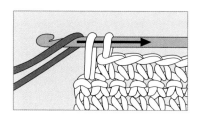

Fig. 3b

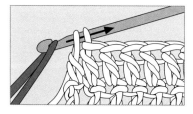

WORKING IN SPACE BEFORE A STITCH

When instructed to work in space **before** a stitch or in spaces **between** stitches, insert hook in space indicated by arrow (*Fig. 5*).

Fig. 5

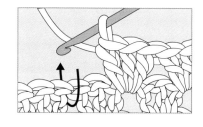

MATTRESS STITCH

With the **right** side of both edges facing you and matching stitches, sew through both sides once to secure the seam. Insert the needle from **back** to **front** through two strands on one side *(Fig. 6a)*, then from **back** to **front** on the other side *(Fig. 6b)*. Continue in this manner drawing seam together as you work. This will create a flat seam.

Fig. 6a

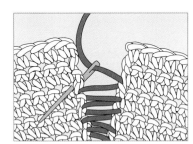

Fig. 6b

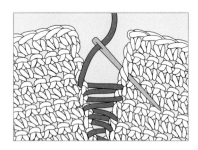

We have made every effort to ensure that these instructions are accurate and complete. We cannot, however, be responsible for human error, typographical mistakes, or variations in individual work.

Production Team: Instructional/Technical Editor - Linda A. Daley; Senior Graphic Artist - Lora Puls; Photo Stylist - Lori Wenger; and Photographer - Jason Masters.

Yarn Information

The Shawls and Scarves in this book were made using Medium and Bulky Weight yarns. Any Medium or Bulky Weight yarn may be used. It is best to refer to the yardage/meters when determining how many balls or skeins to purchase. Remember, to arrive at the finished size, it is the GAUGE/TENSION that is important, not the brand of yarn.

For your convenience, listed below are the yarns used to create our photography models. Because yarn manufacturers make frequent changes in their product lines, you may sometime find it necessary to use a substitute yarn or to search for the discontinued product at alternate suppliers (locally or online).

ALTURAS SHAWL
Lion Brand® Shawl in a Ball®
#307 Cleansing Quartz

IMOGENE INFINITY COWL
Lion Brand® Scarfie
#217 Mint/Silver

TOXAWAY SHAWL
Caron® Simply Soft® Tweeds™
Off White - #23001 Off White
Brown - #23003 Taupe
Caron® Simply Soft®
Orange - #9765 Pumpkin

ALPINE SCARF
Lion Brand® Heartland®
Green - #173 Everglades
Tan - #098 Acadia

TRAIL CREEK SCARF
Bernat® Pop!™
Variegated - #84012 Foggy Notion
Bernat® Pipsqueak™
Off White - #59008 Vanilla

TRINITY CAPELET
Lion Brand® Landscapes®
Gold - #158 Mustard
Lt Grey - #150 Silver

TWIN LAKES INFINITY SCARF
Red Heart® Comfort®
White - #3130 White
Blue - #3152 Denim Heather

Made in U.S.A.